DWELL IN LOVE
II

The Journey of Return

Jerry K. Paul

Copyright © 2004 by Jerry K. Paul

All rights reserved. No part of this book may be reproduced, stored in a retrieval system, or transmitted in any form by any means, whether electronic, mechanical, photocopy, recording or other, without the prior written permission of the author.

Cover photograph of wood carving by Tilman Riemenschneider taken and provided by the late Karl Anslinger. Permission given by Christof Messerschmidt, Pastor, Evangelisches Pfarramt in Creglingen

Published by: *Isaiah Publications*
                P.O. Box 31
                Pine Level, AL 36065
                www.dwellinlove.com

Library of Congress Control Number: 2003108325

ISBN: 0-9741673-1-2

Printed in U.S.A.

ACKNOWLEDGMENTS

First of all I am deeply grateful to our Heavenly Father and our Master, Jesus, for Their great Love for us and for Their patience. I appreciate the fact that they are always willing to provide us with anything that will help us to remember our relationship with Them and to recognize our relationship with our brothers and sisters.

Many thanks to Lynn Sparrow for helping me with attunement and adding her spiritual vibrations to make easier the process of bringing through the messages. Stuart Dean has been the source of priceless support through the years and has inspired me not to place limits on my expectations. My cousin, Mary Roten, has not only encouraged me, but has helped me take care of many of the earthly demands of life so that I would have the time to devote to this work. Thanks also to Tom Baker and Nancy Eubel for helping with two of the messages.

FOREWORD

Dwell in Love II: The Journey of Return is a revolutionary little book. It is revolutionary in the sense that it offers a simple yet profound solution to the problems of the world, both personal and global. It is not about a new movement or institution or organization. It is not even about a startling new revelation or belief system. Rather it is about the power inherent in the heart that seeks to serve humanity in love and humility.

Through an inspiring series of real-life experiences, author Jerry Paul introduces the premise that even the most closed of human hearts may be assisted to open themselves to God's presence through a soul-to-soul meeting with one who holds them up in prayer. There is nothing new about intercessory prayer, but Jerry's approach is predicated upon several key aspects that seem to make the difference between the mundane and the miraculous when it comes to results.

- Jerry begins with a sense of the deep connectedness among all people that makes it genuinely possible for us to communicate directly with any other person at the level of soul, regardless of external boundaries such as geography, personality, culture or religion. Prayer becomes a direct encounter of love with a fellow human being rather than a wish or plea sent up to the heavens.

- The presence of God within all, and the resultant beauty of that presence, is a given in the worldview underlying *Dwell in Love II*. Among the book's most inspiring moments are those when a person previously unaware of his or her divine inner beauty is transformed as a result of having that beauty gently and lovingly coaxed out by the one in intercessory prayer.

- Perhaps most wonderfully of all, the belief that the seeking soul can communicate directly with God and receive detailed, narrative answers forms the inspirational backbone of all that Jerry shares with his readers, both here and in his earlier first volume of *Dwell in Love*. To listen for the voice of God as He responds to the author's prayer-questions reminds the reader that the promise of such close relationship with God is the unopened gift in many of our own lives.

Many readers will be particularly interested in the messages concerning suffering, as this aspect of the human condition is a perennial challenge to the spiritually- and philosophically-inclined. While perhaps we may never fully understand suffering while we are on this earth, this reader couldn't help but feel comforted by the answers that arose from the author's own questing in the presence of his Lord. For those who suffer vicariously on behalf of others, there is very helpful advice to be found here as well.

On the very practical side, the messages Jerry shares about the helpful attributes of various stones and crystals (listed for the reader's convenience in alphabetical order) is yet another reminder of God's love for us and the many ways He has structured the entire world around our awakening to the love and beauty that surrounds and fills us. And, for those who wish to replicate Jerry's experience and join with him in this powerful work of the heart, there is a step-by-step prayer pattern at the end of the first chapter that tells exactly how to give oneself to this form of intercessory prayer.

Finally, on a more personal note, I have had the pleasure of knowing Jerry Paul for nearly a decade now. I have also had the honor of being present for some of the communications he has received and subsequently passed on in his writings to all who care to benefit from them. Having been involved in spiritual and church work since childhood, I have been blessed to meet many good people who earnestly seek to serve God. But Jerry stands out as one of that special group of human beings who truly do "love the Lord their God with all their hearts and minds and souls and their neighbors as themselves." I do believe that for any one of us who combines Jerry's intention of the heart with the practice he describes, the result will be a life transformation – our own and that of the person we are praying for. If enough of us do it, it will change the world. This *is* quite a revolutionary little book.

Lynn Sparrow
January, 2004

TABLE OF CONTENTS

Page

Introduction i

The Journey of Return 3

Message about Serving Those Who Suffer 45

Message about Vicarious Suffering 69

A Reluctant Soul Accepts to Come to Earth 87

God's Gift of Crystals and Stones 101

INTRODUCTION

After finishing my first book, *Dwell in Love*, I asked some friends to read it and give me feedback. Since the material in the book was given to me and not of myself, I really didn't want to add anything else to it; however, after receiving some of the responses, I realized that it is one thing to read a book, and another to put the principles into practice. Because of this, I added a "Note to the Reader" in which I gave two exercises—in hopes it would encourage people to use the ideas in the book in their daily lives. I thought this would be sufficient.

It is true that we often read books about spirituality and find that they present us with beautiful platitudes and spiritual ideas that are difficult to integrate into our own lives. Unless we benefit from them, they are not of much value to us. I was once told that *Dwell in Love* was like a bejeweled city, high in the sky, but with no access ladder. I felt that practicing the exercises *is* the access ladder, and I wasn't very concerned about the comment.

The first paragraph of my "Note to the Reader" in *Dwell in Love* was, "I would like to encourage those who read this book to allow it to inspire them to acknowledge the Spirit of God in all creation and to offer appreciation for it. The results of this will be an experience of Divine Love." One day a friend of mine, who was going through a spiritual and a health crisis, referred to this paragraph and wrote, "I expect to be ill for several years, and most of that time will basically be thrown away. For all the millions of people carrying some such burden, and believing deep in their hearts that the condition is *not* a gift of God, I ask, how do you do this? On a practical level, what do we do? Help us find some way to acknowledge the Spirit of God." This touched me deeply, and in response to that I have written the first chapter in this book. In it I tell of experiences I had, because I think personal experiences make the concepts believable and, therefore, are encouraging. May each person who reads this book be blessed by our Heavenly Father and our beloved Master.

Jerry K. Paul

THE JOURNEY OF RETURN

THE JOURNEY OF RETURN

There is deep within each soul the memory of a purity and perfection it once knew and experienced, and it is this memory that is the lifeline that can lead it back to the full awareness of that state of being. As the soul begins to turn its attention to spiritual things, in the beginning it must rely on hope and belief in this holiness to sustain it. All religions depend on hope and belief as a technique to lift souls up from the stifling hopelessness and despair of pain, suffering, destitution, and total lack of any human love or acts of compassion from other people. Very often the conditions of life are so appalling that the soul is propelled into such beliefs in order to endure the suffering. At times this belief may appear to be an illusion or a state of denial of reality, but without it we truly are hopeless. For those who have not yet grasped for the lifeline of hope and belief it is very difficult, and it is the acknowledgment of Truth at the soul level by those who know It, accompanied by acts of kindness, loving words, and other expressions of our honor for and admiration of our brothers and sisters, that can stir the memory and cause the grip of fear on their hearts to loosen.

It is true that some souls with a deep spiritual awareness may be going through what Christian mysticism calls "The Dark Night of the Soul," and this may cause them to feel as hopeless and lost as those who have not given much thought to spiritual matters. These souls often find it impossible in this state to see that the difficulties in their lives are, in fact, a blessing from God and are designed to bring them closer to Him. Their crying out grips us to the core of our hearts, and yet they must have this experience in order to become free from ego attachment and release themselves totally to God. Here again, it is the privilege and duty of those who know and experience Truth to stand by them in spirit—and often in body. It is one thing to intellectually understand that God only gives us what is best for us, but in the middle of the process of releasing, it is not always possible to feel it deep within. When we are going through these experiences it certainly helps—in fact, it is our salvation—to seek God in our brothers and sisters. In order to experience Divine Love, we must offer it—It fills us while flowing through us. However, it is definitely beneficial to turn to those who know Truth and ask for their support. None of us are whole, perfect, and separate beings unto ourselves, but rather each is a part of the other and of God, and we all have need of communion with each other; therefore, it is our fulfillment—our natural expression—to offer limitless Love and acceptance to each other. It is the support of our brothers *along with* such acts on our own part that carries us through our difficult times.

As we embark upon the journey of returning to the full awareness of our true being, we are often resistant to the very process that is so beneficial. After being brought up in a society that treasures judgment as a sign of intellectual accomplishment and judgment against others as a means of feeling superior to others and aggrandizing our egos, we may at first view relinquishment of judgment and seeking to discover the Spirit of God in other people as an obstacle. We may even say, "I don't want to see God in this person whom I dislike. I just want to experience God by Himself." It does take some use of the intellect and a step of faith to accept that what we observe with our earthly senses is the expression of the ego, which is not perfect, and that there is a perfection beyond these perceptions that can be discovered. One must surely want to become aware of this reality in order to accept to use certain techniques in order to achieve the goal. For some people—especially religious people—it may come as a surprise to hear that use of the imagination (in the appropriate way, of course) can be a very powerful spiritual tool. To imagine perfection to be where we had judged it impossible to be is the first step in reinterpreting all those things we have judged against. It is certainly much easier in the beginning to imagine this when we are alone in a meditative state, because the personality of other people is so strong as to cause us to put up barriers when we are in their physical presence.

For those who just don't find within themselves the desire or willingness to do this on their own, if there is any desire to do it at all, there is every possible help available from God. We need only ask, and He will arrange everything in the perfect way and at the appropriate time, and He has tremendous joy when we ask Him for help. We are, after all, His children—a part of Himself—and His love for us is indescribable. We must of course accept that the methods He uses may not seem to have any value to us—simply because we don't understand the process. When we ask in earnest, then we must accept whatever presents itself to us, and at least give it a try.

If we ask God for help, He will begin to present us with events, circumstances, and encounters that encourage and inspire us to persevere. We may hear of books, workshops, stories of experiences other people have had, etc. One of the most memorable things He gave me was a beautiful dream. I will relate it to show how moving one of His gifts was.

DREAM OF LIGHT

During the early 1970's I had several dreams of searching for a secret staircase. About 1:00 a.m. on November 30, 1974, I awoke after having a dream that was my first intense spiritual experience. I dreamt that I was going up and down some stairway seeking a secret passage. Someone came and told me to wait, and he would go get the key. When he returned I saw him unlock some golden gates. I was aware of where I had just come from, and, as it were, stepped back to that place. Immediately I was told by others to go back (I would otherwise lose the lofty state of consciousness). I returned and ascended some steps to what appeared to be a stage, and entered into a very lofty, royal hall furnished with gold and with beautiful draperies. I felt that I was approaching the Presence of God. The level of consciousness was very high, but suddenly it dropped back to where I had been, and the splendor began to fade. I fought to blot out the lower vibrations and regain the splendor, much as a drowning person fights to regain the surface of water. It was granted me to regain that high level. I then noticed an old man, who might have been an overseer (such as Saint Peter).

Suddenly I turned around to look behind me and encountered an intensely bright light, which I could not bear. I felt that I was in the Presence of God and threw myself on my face. I heard a voice deep within me ask God to never let me stray from the way to Him, to make me pure, and to make me of service to my fellowman. It seemed that the awesome presence was on a balcony, such as those above the entrance to Gothic cathedrals. I never saw a figure there—I was just aware of blinding Light and indescribable splendor. Then as the splendor began to fade, I fought again to regain the high level of consciousness. I was shown a beautiful curtain closing on a very high, but rather narrow stage, and the word "Pluto" was written across the curtain.

For many years I pondered the meaning of the word, "Pluto." In the mid 1990's I was under a lot of stress with my job and caring for both of my elderly and sick parents, in addition to my sister who had had problems from brain damage since birth. I kept saying to myself, "I'm being destroyed." Then I read two books by Bernadette Roberts called *The Path of No-Self* and *The Experience of No-Self*. I realized that No-Self is when the ego has been destroyed, but a shell of it continues because that is necessary for us here on earth. This destruction of the ego was what the word "Pluto" symbolized.

TURNING OBSTACLES INTO BLESSINGS

As mentioned above, resistance to seeking to recognize the Spirit of God in others can be a major obstacle for some people. I understand that well because I was one of those who said, "I don't want to see God in other people. I just want to experience the Presence of God." I had spent many years reading various books about spiritual development and mysticism. Some of the books I didn't even understand, and others offered techniques that were impossible for me to use; such as, stilling the mind of all thoughts. The idea of communing with God by seeking Him in other people seemed novel, but a bit off the mark. I dismissed the idea at first, but events in my life had brought me to a spiritual and emotional crisis. This state was necessary in order for me to accept the ideas God had presented to me, and that I had rejected. The following shows how I was saved from the dilemma.

JESUS IN THE THEATER

It was spring 1982. My life had been a series of failures for many years. I had been unable to finish my studies as a musician because of joint problems. I was studying data processing, but didn't really like it. I was depressed because, after many years of intensely studying spiritual material of various sorts, I still felt as though God was far away and not hearing or responding to me. I never found any way of communing with Him, and he always seemed silent when I talked to Him. I told Him that I didn't think I could take it any more. During spring break I had state and federal income taxes to complete for three people, as well as a list of other things to do. A very spiritual friend of mine called and said that he wanted to visit—that he had been told in prayer that he should come. I couldn't say "No," but I really didn't have the time.

One evening we were sitting and talking about spiritual things, and I told him that I had sunk as far as I could go in what had seemed to be a bottomless pit. As I was talking I noticed a light in him, and I knew it wasn't something I was seeing with my physical eyes, but I disregarded it. As we continued to talk, I noticed it again a couple more times. I thought it was strange, but I didn't have time to think about it or try to sort it out. One day he said, "Let's go to a movie." I said, "I don't have time. I've got to get these tax papers finished." He said, "I'll drive and you can work on them while we are in the car." (It was a drive of about thirty miles.) So, again reluctantly, I agreed. As it turned out, the movie we were going to see was Chariots of Fire, *which had a strong spiritual tone to it.*

After the movie had been going about half an hour, I suddenly noticed that Jesus was sitting next to me in the body of my friend. I knew without a doubt that it was Jesus, but it seemed so strange. I kept looking at my friend, who seemed engrossed in the movie. The sense of the Presence of Jesus and the Divine Love he was sending me was so strong I couldn't ignore or doubt it. I had been drinking a lot of water and got up to go to the restroom several times, and every time I returned, Jesus was still there. I think that my state of despair made the Presence even more overpowering. After we left the theater I couldn't help but weep, even in the presence of my friend. Finally, I had experienced that God and Jesus did love me and had not forgotten me.

After returning home I mentioned to my friend that I had noticed a light in him several times earlier, and he told me that he had been concentrating on the Spirit of God in me rather than accepting as reality my description of my deplorable state of being. He then helped me to begin to seek to experience the Presence of God in other people, rather than just abstractly by trying to still my mind—which I definitely could not do—and experience God for myself alone. I will always be grateful to my friend for accepting to be God's vessel to help me at a time when I really wasn't seeking help anymore, as well as helping me during the years since that time. He was an example to me of a vessel being always willing and ready to go where God sends him, no matter what the circumstances are. Thank you, dear brother!

This was a wonderful experience, and it gave me hope again, but we cannot just simply revel in these glorious experiences and consider that there is nothing beyond them. God gives them to us in order to encourage us as we continue to allow all those things that block our view of Him and the reality of our brothers and sisters to be peeled away one by one. If we actively participate in the process, progress is much faster. Because my despair had been so great and my desire to know God continued with intensity, I was willing to seek to have experiences of His Presence over and over again—in spite of resistance from the ego. This is how it began.

EXPERIENCE OF ONENESS

Shortly after the experience of Jesus' Presence in the theater, I had been thinking about the experience of being at-one with others, which is sometimes described by spiritual people. My parents had an old country store, one that sold just about everything—groceries, some drug items, work clothes, shoes, hardware, feed for all sorts of livestock, gasoline, and limited car parts. One day my parents, an aunt who helped us, and I were all there, and an old, very poor, and illiterate man came in. He was unusually grumpy that day—nothing satisfied him. As I was standing watching what was going on, I whispered to God: "I would like to experience my oneness with this man." In an instant I felt truly one with him. I wasn't used to getting, or at least recognizing, such a quick response from God. Maybe it was because I had bounced back from being so low in the bottomless pit and was now interested in experiencing God in someone other than myself. I was standing thinking about this when the old man, who had finished his shopping, started to leave. As he passed by, he turned to me and, in his colloquial dialect, said, "You know, pretty boy, sometimes I'm a little fussy, but I really like you." I knew immediately that my experience of oneness was not just mine—he had also experienced something. As I began seeking to commune with the Spirit of God in other people, I came to realize that the blessing was one shared by both of us.

Truly, an experience of holiness is worth more than a thousand books on the subject. One experience alone is enough to cause us to begin to ask to know God in all people, circumstances, and situations around us, and as we do this, the obstacle of resistance begins to melt. Still, at first it is much easier to want to see God in people for whom we have no negative feelings. There is more resistance when feelings of fear or dislike are attached. Such feelings are interpretations and perceptions based on limited earthly knowledge, or in many cases simply hearsay. It takes a certain boldness to be willing to say to God, "I feel no love for or attraction to this person, but I am willing to allow You to show me the truth."

DEATH ROW INMATE

I now often choose to seek the Spirit of God in people whom my personality would like most to reject, but at first this wasn't easy. I do a lot of talking in my prayer and meditation sessions. I speak to the people of the beauty of the Spirit of God within them and ask them to open the door of their hearts and bless me with an experience of God's Love there.

In the 1980's there was much publicity in my state about a death row inmate who had committed a heinous crime and was about to be put to death. If I recall correctly, he robbed a store, and then shot and killed the owner in front of the owner's child. It was said that he had no remorse whatsoever. I think it was the day before the scheduled execution that I decided to include this young man in my prayers. Much to my surprise, I received a beautiful wave of indescribable love. I was so blessed and overjoyed by it!

After the execution had taken place, the news commentators said that before being executed, the young man said that he was sorry about the crime he had committed, knew that he deserved the punishment he was about to receive, and was at peace. I don't know what had brought him to that point, but I think it is because of this that he was so open to me the night before his death. I thank him for the blessing he gave me!

As time went on I began to think that I should extend my communing to include more people whom I had never met, and those who could have a great effect on circumstances in the world. I have found that often when I start working with someone, it seems the door is bolted and no one is at home. It takes about a week before they even seem to begin to listen to what I am saying to them.

WORLD FIGURES

Some time in the late 1980's, when the news often featured stories about Gorbachev and Ayatollah Khomeini, I decided to commune with the Spirit of God in them. It took a lot of patience and effort—prayer/meditation can sometimes be very hard work. At first, Gorbachev seemed as if he were in a deepfreeze, but as the months went by he seemed to thaw. I spoke often to him in spirit, telling him of the beautiful Spirit of Light within him and urging him to allow it to beam forth from him into all the world. As time went by we certainly did see that he did that. The collective prayers of all of us surely helped him to do it.

As for the Ayatollah, it was a very different story, and it serves to show how uniquely each one of us was created by our Heavenly Father. I began my attempts to commune with him around New Year of that year—1989 I think it was. I spoke similar things to him and urged him to accept the great opportunity he had to spread God's Light into the world. About five months later, one night as I was focusing on the Divine Light in his heart, suddenly he opened the door of his heart and allowed me to see his true being. What I beheld was a beautiful, brilliant, and still light. I was so blessed by the experience that several days later I realized that every time I thought of him I only thought of that beautiful light. Then I also realized that he was the first person whom I had ever totally forgiven, for now I didn't think of him as being what I had judged him to be. One evening a couple of days later, as I was walking through the family room, the news was on, and I heard the commentator say, "Ayatollah Khomeini has said that even though it is bitter as medicine, he will agree to talk peace with Iraq." I continued to commune with him, and one evening he raised his arms and embraced me as his brother. As he raised his arms in spirit his right arm brushed my left side, and I actually felt it in my body.

Often we need to have our fears brought to our attention in order to prod us to seek to know God in all circumstances and accept that our responsibility does not end with ourselves. As strange as it may seem, it is sometimes easier to desire to see God and know His Presence in those who turn us off than in those with whom we have some very positive and intimate relationship. If we dislike someone, we may simply want to see something better, but if we love what we perceive on the earthly level, we have no desire to go beyond that. Yet, when those whom we love suffer, we are propelled to reach deeper within ourselves and bring forth the desire to make even those relationships holy. Such was the case with my mother.

MY MOTHER

My mother had been through great suffering with a knee replacement and then a hip replacement, followed by a split in the bone around the artificial hip joint. She had always been a very strong person who felt that she could do anything. She was very active in church work and loved to bake. Everything had to be baked from scratch, and it was absolutely delicious. Now she was very weak and depressed. She would only lie on the couch all day and do nothing. I attempted to commune with her for a whole year, but it seemed the door to her heart was bolted. About five days after the experience with Ayatollah Khomeini, she suddenly flung open the doors of her heart, and the Light there washed over me in great waves that made me laugh. I was amazed and struck by how different the Light was from that in Khomeini, which was so serene. The next afternoon when I came home from work, I noticed freshly baked pastries on the kitchen table. She was back at it, and we were delighted.

When people don't respond, it is often tempting to give up. It is very difficult to continue to go to the door of the person's heart day after day—whispering to them and coaxing them to allow you to see the beauty of the Light there and to experience the joy of their love—when you get no response, but the patience and confidence we have is well worth the wait and also is a test of our love for them. I find the endurance comes when I say, "I thank you, Father, that You come to me as this dear brother (or sister) to bless me with Your Love."

The obstacles of resistance become less and less as we enter into holy embraces more and more. Based on the memory of past experiences we know that the mask of personality, which sometimes is somewhat frightening, always covers love and beauty. We may spend a number of years focusing on healing relationships with other people before we begin to realize that there are many more layers that need to be peeled away. We must eventually extend the relinquishment of judgment and perception to all facets of our lives. An opportunity was presented to me to do this with a dog.

LADY

I went to visit some friends in Virginia one summer, and after arriving, one of my friends said to me, "I have a friend who has an old dog by the name of Lady to whom she is very attached. Lady is very sick with pancreatitis, and the veterinarian has suggested euthanasia. Would you pray for Lady?" I agreed, but wondered how best to do it. I went into my room, folded my knees, and sat down on my feet. I had no idea what kind of dog it was or what she looked like. I just pretended there was a dog on the floor in front of me and started talking to her. I told her that God is present in everything that exists, and His Light is also in her. I concentrated on the Light of God that was within her and gave thanks for It. When I was finished I seemed to sense the presence of the dog and was a little surprised that she didn't jump on me and lick me as dogs like to do. It seemed that she just sat there and looked at me rather lady like.

The next day I was hurriedly getting dressed to go somewhere, and suddenly it seemed that Lady was there, sitting on the floor looking up at me. Since I was in a hurry, I didn't think much about it and just said, "Hello, Lady." The following day I was brushing my teeth and again in a hurry to go someplace when, suddenly, there was Lady sitting on the floor before me and looking at me. Again I just said, "Hello, Lady," and rushed to finish and leave. The third day after praying for Lady was the day before I was to return home. A friend and I were sitting quietly in a restaurant after ordering our meal, and suddenly, there was Lady again. This time I was not in a hurry and couldn't help but laugh, and of course I explained to my friend why I was laughing. After I had returned home, I called to let my friends know that I had arrived home safely, and my friend said to me, "I just talked to my friend who owns Lady. She said that Lady is healed, and the veterinarian says it is a miracle."

In my experiences with prayer, I have found that often children and pets respond more quickly than adults. Perhaps it is because they are more open to accepting an acknowledgment of God's Presence and to accepting unconditional love from another person.

Regardless of how spiritual we may think we are or how often we experience God's Presence, there come times of dearth—times when most people don't seem to be responding as we approach them in spirit—and we wonder if we are doing something wrong. Such times can be discouraging, but even in times of famine God sustains us and keeps us from losing hope (See I Kings 17:8-16). It can even be delightful.

EXPERIENCES WITH A CHILD

I have two beautiful friends who had a son born in the mid-seventies. I saw him the day he was born and was amazed at how alert and aware he seemed. I later moved from the area and only had a chance to see them about twice a year. On one of my visits when the child was about three years old, he was sitting on my lap watching cartoons, and I began to feel his spirit reaching out to me. On the personality level he was being entertained by the cartoons, but on a deeper level there was a communing of the spirits within us and an exchange of a beautiful love. From that time on there seemed to be a strong bond between us—that is, until the age of puberty hit, and, as some teenagers do, he shut down for a few years.

Sometimes, when he was still small, my friends would say to me on the telephone, "He is being obnoxious and won't cooperate. Will you pray for him?" When I did my evening prayer and meditation, I called him by name, and immediately I could feel him come running to me, jump on me, and throw his arms around my neck. The next day my friends would say that he was totally different. This little friend was always ready to exchange love. I even called him "my old faithful" because, if I was having a very dry prayer and meditation period, all I had to do was call his name and have an exchange of the Love of God in our spirits. It was so uplifting! A couple of times when I was sitting at work I felt him come to me in spirit, hovering above my left shoulder. I would pause a moment to receive his love and reciprocate.

I think this beautiful child helped me to understand more than anyone else how much difference it makes when we take the time and make the effort to seek to recognize the Spirit of God in others. Our brothers and sisters need it, and so do we. I personally think this is both the best and the easiest way to commune with God and be mindful of Him in our lives.

Often times we go through life with the desire to be mindful of God, and yet at the end of a day we may say, "I was so caught up in all the activities that I didn't even think of God." We recognize that it is the things we dislike or the things that challenge us that awaken us to the need to look beyond the outer nature and recognize God there. This can range from unpleasant situations to an illness that disables us. We may find it difficult to acknowledge such things as a blessing, but if we reflect upon it, we will realize that we seek God most when things are difficult. Even a minor irritation can result in a blessing for many people if we allow it to be a reminder to look for Truth and seek to experience Love by offering It.

SPIRIT OF GOD IN THE PULPIT

I once attended a church where the minister really loved to talk about the Love of God, and when he did so, you could feel that he knew what he was talking about. There came a point in time when he was going through a lot of stress and difficulty, and one Sunday morning he was giving us a tongue-lashing of a sermon. I wouldn't say that we didn't deserve it, but after about fifteen minutes of being scolded, I was getting weary of it. I looked at his heart area and started focusing on the Light of God there so intensely that I wasn't seeing anything else. After I had done this about five minutes, he suddenly stopped—it seemed as if in mid-sentence—turned, and looked at me for a couple of seconds. Then his voice took on a very gentle and loving tone, and the rest of the sermon was inspiringly beautiful.

I might also add that when this minister would lead a prayer for someone who was sick or in trouble, he would often say, "Father, we lift them up into Your arms." I think that was extremely powerful, because I can imagine that everyone was visualizing lifting that person into God's arms.

There has been some discussion in spiritual circles about the appropriateness of praying for things for the physical body, and some people think it should not be done. I have received messages from God and Jesus indicating that the physical, emotional, and mental parts of our being should not be looked down upon or neglected. Of course, we must keep the proper perspective. Jesus once said, "Seek ye first the kingdom of God, and his righteousness; and all these things shall be added unto you." (Matt 6:33) To me this means that we first turn to God, seek His Holy Presence, and acknowledge that all gifts come from Him. We ask that He grant that which will draw us closer to Him, and we desire that only His Will be done. When other people ask us to pray for them, we seek the Spirit of God in them and ask the same thing. Sometimes immediate relief is not God's answer, but again, we can be surprised.

A HEALING

Some years ago a friend of mine had a problem with his stomach. It was severe enough that the doctor decided to perform a procedure by which my friend had to be anesthetized and have an instrument inserted through the mouth into the stomach. It seemed there was some concern that he might have an ulcer, or even cancer of the stomach. For a couple of days I tried to commune with the Spirit of God in him, but got no response. On the night before the procedure I stood before the door of my friend's heart in spirit talking to him about the beauty of that spirit within. I asked him to open the door and allow the Spirit of God there to bless me, but it seemed the door of his heart was bolted. Finally, I said, "You can ignore me if you like, but if you think I'm going away, you are wrong. I'm going to stay here until you open the door." After about five minutes, suddenly he flung open the door of his heart and allowed God to bless me with a wave of Divine Love. I gave thanks and knew that my friend had released himself to God, and all would go according to God's Will.

The next evening I called to find out the results of the test. When my friend answered the telephone, I asked "What did they find?" He replied, "Nothing, but I had a healing." I said, "What do you mean?" He answered, "I had been told that for a certain number of hours before the procedure I couldn't take any kind of medication. Last night I had a terrible sinus headache that wasn't getting any better. Finally, I decided to soak in a tub of hot water. As I lay there in the water I had a healing, and I knew you had something to do with it."

Our problems and illnesses are usually symptoms of the "disconnect" between our consciousness and the awareness of our true being, but they must be approached from the very root of their existence; in other words, they are most effectively worked on from the inside outwards, rather than vice versa.

Sometimes in our frustration with conditions in our lives and those of our brothers and sisters we may feel as though we would like to storm the gates of heaven, but that really does not work. We can't force entry into the hearts of others, but if we stand by them faithfully, radiating a gentle love, they will, with time, notice how non-threatening we are, and eventually release their fear. It is our privilege and also a source of great spiritual blessings when we do this. Jesus told his disciples. "This is my commandment, that ye love one another as I have loved you." (John 15:12)

MESSAGE FROM THE MASTER
CHRISTMAS DAY 2003

I have asked our dear Master to bless us with a message on this joyous day.

Come unto me, all you who are heavily laden with burdens of the body, heart, mind, and soul, and I will surely help. If you will only ask Me, and then release the burden to me, I will find the perfect solution to every situation. You do not know the perfect solution—what would be most beneficial to you—but if you will trust Me, you will receive relief, Peace, and Joy. If symptoms and signs continue for a short span, do not give up hope. Remember that in order to receive relief from a splinter embedded in the flesh, you must first endure having it removed before the healing process can begin. If you had only an inkling of My Love for you, you would know that My Father and I do not punish and have no delight in seeing you suffer, but we do know the process of making you whole again—healing you from your fragmented state of awareness. Do the following:

1. *Approach the Father and Me without fear.*
2. *Ask of Us (speak to us of your concerns—what is troubling you).*
3. *Leave the burden with Us (don't carry it back in your heart, or come back later and try to get it so that you can carry it around with you).*
4. *Trust (accept that We will arrange everything according to your best interest).*
5. *Give thanks that the burden is no longer yours—allow your joy to be seen in your countenance.*
6. *Look for opportunities to allow Us to extend Love through you to others.*
7. *Accept gladly the circumstances of those opportunities, even though from an earthly perspective they may seem to inconvenience you.*

Understand that difficult circumstances may be the needle that removes the splinter of obstacles you have carried for eons. Those of you who know of Me know that I have always extended Love. If you are in a difficult situation, close your eyes and imagine Me as I was on earth—imagine that you are in My Presence. Speak to me of what concerns you, and then allow yourself to feel and accept the Love with which you must surely know, without a doubt, I envelop you. Your little step of faith and trust, which is not unfounded, is all that is asked of you. The rest is Our job. If you find your faith wavering, turn to one who knows Me well, and ask him or her to speak to you of Me. Remind yourself every day that I am in your heart and stand ever beside you.

Forget not your brothers and sisters, for I tell you, no one comes before Our Father or Me in love and asking for the sake of others without finding entry. Devotion to your fellowman allows the door to be opened, for devotion is that Spirit of the Father within you coming into your awareness. Do accept that there is no greater purpose than this to be on earth, and release the goals of the ego, for they will never satisfy you. Every day state that your intention is to be a vessel of the Father, pure and empty, so that He may through you call your wandering and confused brothers and sisters *back to Him. As you think of them, touch each one in spirit with love, and give thanks unto the Father for the opportunity to know His Love flowing through you to them.*

Now, go with the blessings of the Father and Myself. Your brothers and sisters are waiting for you! Many will only know and experience Our Love through you.

A WAY OF PRAYING

I certainly do not intend to try to improve on the Master's message, but I thought it was important to first share His message before going to this next topic. I have resisted the suggestions of several people to give exercises because I felt that sharing my experiences would be the best way of assisting those who care to try the approach to spirituality that has been so helpful to me; however, again a personal situation has touched my heart, and I have decided to suggest a way of praying that works very well for me.

If there is a situation bothering you that involves another person, I would suggest that you go to the Father and the Master using the steps He so lovingly gave. We should always speak of these things with Them, and most of us don't have a problem with that. A little more difficult is leaving the burden with Them, trusting, and giving thanks for something of which we have not yet seen the manifestation. What I am going to suggest has already been related, but in order to be of most assistance, I will gather the ideas together all in one place.

1. If possible, sit quietly in a place where there won't likely be any interruptions and try to release the cares of the world. Taking a few deep breaths sometimes helps.
2. Approach the Father and the Master and be perfectly honest about your feelings. If there is a situation you are concerned about—someone is sick, someone has hurt you or saddened you, or if you just really hate someone, admit it. God already knows anyway, but you need to face your feelings yourself. If you do not feel like loving or forgiving the person, tell God about it, but then *ask Him to help you to be willing to release these feelings to Him and accept to see things differently*. This is the key that unlocks the bolted door of your heart. God will not force entry, but if you ask for help, that unlocks the door and leaves it slightly ajar so that He can help.

3. Now, imagine that person is standing in front of you. Think of the body and personality of him or her. Then accept in your mind that God has come to you to bless you, but He is wearing the body and personality of that person as a mask. Imagine the mask becoming thinner and transparent, and behind it is a Purity, a Holiness, and an indescribable Love that could only be coming straight from the Heart of God. Consider yourself to be in the Presence of God, and never think that you need to fear It. Remember, God *is* Love. (When you imagine God's Presence, you allow those things that block your vision and experience of It to fade because it is the perception that He is not there that blocks the experience.)
4. After you have accepted that this is true, and can begin to feel the beauty of the experience of being there, now, talk to God. Tell Him how much you adore Him and how thankful you are that He is Love and you can always approach Him.
5. Say, "I thank you, dear Father, that You have come to me this day as (the person's name) to bless me with an experience of being in Your Presence and knowing

Your Love." Pause a moment and allow yourself to be blessed—linger in the experience of it. (You receive by giving, i.e., you experience God's Presence as His Love flows through that person to you, and it happens because you have acknowledged His Presence there and offered appreciation for It.)

6. Then you might ask God to also help that person to experience His Love just as you have experienced It.

7. It could be that God may place into your mind an idea of something you could do. Sometimes when a person is sick, worried, or depressed, I may get a feeling that there is negative energy around him like a cloud, and I may feel prompted to say, "All that is not in accordance with the Father's will for you at this time, if you allow, I will remove." Then I imagine that I am gathering it in my arms, and I place it over a Flame of Divine Love beside me, so that the dross can be burned away and release the pure energy of God to bless us all in the way it was intended.

8. Allow your heart to open, and your love to envelop the person.

9. Now give thanks for the situation that has brought you to this experience. Admit to yourself that if you had not had difficulty, you might not have taken the time to seek out God. Try to accept that what brought the situation on was really a way of that person reaching out for love (if he felt loved the situation would not have come about), and now you have both been blessed because *you* didn't stumble over the situation, but rather accepted to use it as a tool to look beyond it.

MESSAGE ABOUT SERVING THOSE WHO SUFFER

MESSAGE ABOUT SERVING THOSE WHO SUFFER

We have been told that at times suffering serves a purpose of causing us to seek the Father and help awaken us from our spiritual sleep; however, it often seems that people who are suffering are devastated by hopelessness and pain. We ask the Heavenly Father to instruct us as to how we can best allow Him to extend blessings of Hope, Love, and Peace through us to those who are suffering so that we may assist our brothers without supporting their illusions or prolonging the process of liberation.

It is always My great joy when children of Mine approach Me and desire to be instruments through which their brothers who are suffering may receive some relief, as well as be brought into a closer communion with Me. And it is those who come desiring to be totally empty through whom I can best send forth those blessings. I would ask you always to come first to Me. Ask Me for those blessings that would benefit them the most. Do not decide for yourself that they simply need relief from suffering, but ask for that which will bring them closer to Me. Be always willing and ready to drop those mundane things that may seem to interest you to some extent—to drop those and go at My bidding. And remember always, when you look upon those brothers, you may at first see suffering, you may see delusion and ignorance, but look past that quickly—look past that at My Spirit within. And when you see that Spirit of Mine there in all Its Beauty, Its Light, Its Purity, radiating Its Love to you, you receive My blessings, and you can be assured that those brothers of yours in whom you see My Spirit will always be blessed by the very fact that you look beyond that mask, and look at the true Being that is there, which is Myself extended. This is the blessing that you can offer to your brothers, and it also brings you the greatest blessing you can have, which is a conscious communion with Me, bringing joy into your heart. Now, after this has been done, then listen quietly, for I may tell you other things. And be not speedy in trying to be about doing good works. Wait patiently, so that I may you show exactly what your brothers need, and at the time when it is perfect for them to receive it. Be assured that this will take place. Have no doubts that, when you come in love, wanting to be of service to your brothers, it will happen. And always remember, those blessings that are offered—your recognition, you're appreciation for what you see there, your recognition of My Spirit there—will always be a blessing for them, which may take a little bit of time—as you see it on earth—to manifest. But it will come. It is not possible that you would come to Me with love, asking for your brothers to be conscious of and to experience My Love as you do, and this would not happen. I bless you—I bless all who desire to do this in My Name.

Go forth as My obedient children—always extending love and always accepting, realizing, that your brothers are on a pathway towards Me; and it does not matter where on the pathway they are—they are on the way. And when you acknowledge Me within them, you help to turn them away from those things that distract them, and turn them facing towards Me, so that they may proceed and be liberated from those things that cause them to feel alienated, to feel not loved, to feel lost, to feel pain—those things that cause them to suffer. Remember also, there are those who suffer in ways other than physical suffering. Often they bring this about themselves by their own thoughts, their own attitudes, their own doubts. And at other times this suffering that is other than physical is, or appears to be, brought on by other brothers. But even this can be a great blessing and should not be perceived as being a punishment, but that which will cause them to turn to Me looking for their answers—rather than looking for answers in places where they really cannot be found. Go forth with this as your purpose. Your purpose is to be of assistance to your brothers, and that is a very high purpose for anyone on the earth at this time of harvest.

It has been said a number of times that earth is a place where souls come to grow in awareness of spiritual things and of God by making choices, and it is necessary that they have these choices; therefore, it would not serve the divine plan to have negative forces removed. Please tell us how we can best inspire our brothers, or allow You to inspire them through us, to make the choice for Light, Love, and Oneness, rather than for separation, domination, and selfishness, so that we can do our part in having them provided with every possible opportunity to choose that which brings life, joy, and consciousness of the relationship with their Heavenly Father.

Even many of those who appear to be so cold and ruthless are often touched at a very deep level by an act of kindness, a soft and gentle response. And this can awaken in them a very deep knowing, a recognition, that there is another way, and that what they really seek is to know and experience the relationship with the Father. But remember also that the act of kindness and the gentle and loving response does not have to be delivered from one physical form to another. When you, in the quietness of your devotional period, come before Me in spirit bringing your brothers with you, you have not in any lesser way served them or your purpose on earth. For as you come in spirit with them, with your arms around them, many times this is even the best way that they can be served because, on a deeper level, they hear what you say, they feel how you yourself feel towards them, and it stirs them very deeply within—on a level deeper than the personality level, which would in some cases not respond to an act of kindness or a gentle word.

So, continue coming before Me many times during the day when you have a moment of quietness, and it may just be half a minute—you think of someone, you think of your brothers in other countries and what they are going through. Think of them; bring them without any inhibition with you before Me and ask that they be blessed. Ask that they be helped to accept the blessing that I have in store for them. Ask always to be the vessel and the instrument. Ask Me to provide more and more opportunities for more and more brothers, so that they may be helped. This is your purpose. This is your assignment. This is why you are here—you and so many of your other brothers. Just remember not to be so caught up with things of earth that you might neglect to do this, for My prompting to you will often be very subtle and very gentle, and you may find yourself having to make a choice: "Do I continue to run this errand right now, or do I pause a moment?" Remember also always, what is most important is your brothers and their relationship with Me, and what you can do, or allow to be done through you, to assist them. For as you do this you are truly an extension of Myself expressing in Its true and natural way and manner, rather than being distracted.

We ask the Heavenly Father and Jesus to speak to us about what part Jesus plays in world affairs and how we might intervene in His name, if at all.

You are not aware, but He stands beside the leaders of the countries who will listen, and He even comes and stands beside those leaders who have not listened, urging them in every way possible to seek to extend love and to allow Me, through them, to bring about this spreading of love and the relinquishment of self-centeredness, selfishness, in all manners in which it expresses—trying to dominate, suppress, and harm other brothers. He stands there waiting, just hoping for anyone to turn and say, "Help me, just show me the way, just lead me, just put the thoughts in my mind, just open the avenues for those things that are the Will of the Father." He is always there, and the part that you can play is always to pray for those leaders in particular—not that they are more important than the other brothers, but because the position they have on earth makes their decisions have an impact on a greater number of people. Remember those leaders and come in love with your arms around them, talking to them of the Heavenly Father's Love, speaking to them of the great opportunity they each have to allow the Light to be spread through them and allow an experience of My Love to also come to those in the countries where they have their influence. This is your role. They have theirs, but you support them with your prayers. All brothers need to remember to do this, for it has great effect. And those leaders who will not listen will, after a certain length of time, be removed from those positions. If you continue to pray and continue to ask for Light and Love, your brothers will have their liberation and will be relieved of those who are oppressing them.

A teacher once said that it is essential for us to be able to see in our brothers what we would worship in God. What was he talking about?

Stop and think about it. What would you seek in your Father? You seek unconditional love. You seek a glimpse of purity, of holiness. You seek One who cares for everyone, and as you seek that in your brother, you are not just pretending. You may use your imagination to open the door, but as soon as that door opens, you really do see and experience this—you feel it because I am there in your brother. It is My Spirit that gives your brother his life, so seek that and all things that you would seek in Me! When you come before Me in your prayer, what do you expect from Me? Seek that in your brother. You can look for that in him, and you may be astounded that you receive through your brother the answers to whatever you have asked of Me. You will be amazed at the words that are spoken through his mouth. You will also sometimes be amazed at the acts of kindness and the deeds you receive from him. I may lead you into situations where you need the help of another brother because you are at a place where you cannot do what needs to be done for yourself on even the most physical level. And then you find that a brother appears, one whom you might think to be the least likely, and you know that it is I, come to you—it is I who have assisted you. And you change your mind about your brother simply because you have accepted to look for Me in him, and to receive your blessings through him rather than to bypass him and ask that you receive them directly from Me without having your brothers involved. You cannot leave them out. They are a part of you; they are a part of Me. You must extend your arms and embrace them all, and wait for the conscious recognition of that to come about in all of them. But just continue to do this.

So are you My child, and so do I have My great joy in you always.

Please comment on prophecies of upcoming change.

As the world goes through its cleansing processes, there will be wars and rumors of wars, as you have been told before. But this is a process of cleansing, and as more and more of darkness is washed away, you will see more and more of My Light. It takes your participation for this to happen, but the darkness may be washed away—even as you bring your brothers one by one before Me, and you first just gently remove some of the darker clouds you see around them so that they not be so clouded and not be so burdened, and can come easily with you before Me and rejoice in it. Each one of these acts brings about more quickly the time when earth will shine as a brilliant star, and the negativity and darkness is parted away. As to the exact time when this comes about, that will not be given, for it depends in part on you doing your part, playing your role. But of course there is a time when these things must be, according to My Will—there is just some leeway there as to how quickly it comes about, depending upon your participation. But look forward to the Light. Always look forward to the Light. Do your part to bring it into the earth, so that this may come about, for in envisioning this and asking to be allowed to participate, you bring it about much more quickly. Do not dwell upon the appearances of darkness, for you slow down the process that way. Just look for Light. Everywhere you turn look for Light, express Light, let it beam forth from your eyes, let it be known in the tone of the laughter of your voice, and in that which you speak. For if you will allow it, I speak through you, and it is not possible that your brothers would not be touched, in some way, at some point in time.

How can the vessel best serve the Father in regard to other people's requests for help?

The first step is to come before Me. Do not assume that you know how to do anything. All of the things that you have done to prepare yourself do not take the place of coming before Me. They just give you tools through which you can more quickly allow Me to work through you. You come before Me and just simply say, "My dear Father, I care about my brother, or sister. I desire that he, or she, receive all blessings that can be received and are appropriate at this time. I desire that each one know your Presence, for just hearing about your Presence is not sufficient—I desire that each one experience Your Love, and whatever appears to be oppressing them be lifted. And now, help me to be Your empty vessel, so that You may bless my brothers." And then, just simply wait until I put the ideas into your mind, until I speak through you, until I present a situation that needs to be acted upon. And as your brothers come to you, just look for Me there. Remember, as you do unto them, you do unto Me. And as you recognize the beauty of the spirit within them—the true reality of what they are—you allow all things, and this is the best thing that you can do. You do not have to prepare some written message or some technique, for I will use what is the appropriate message or technique for each one, and it will differ from day to day. Just prepare yourself in any way that may seem appropriate, so that you may have those tools at hand, and then just wait for me to pull out the tool and remind you, "This is a tool, and it is the perfect one for this brother." And just bless him, just extend your love and allow him to feel enveloped in My Love, and this will cause all things to melt away in the experience of being in My Presence.

Please instruct the vessel as to how to go about preparing to serve when others request help, i.e., what to say, how to say it, how much to plan ahead of time, and how much to expect to be given in the moment.

It is always well to prepare yourself in whatever way that you may know, and that may seem appropriate at the time you are preparing, for in that way you have all the tools lined up in front of you. And then when you stand before your brothers, do not feel that you are confined to this list or to the order in which the tools are lined up. You have prepared yourself, so that all you have to do when I put the message into your mind is just pull out this drawer and open it up, pull out this book, this paragraph, this sentence, and it will flow through you because you have done all that you know how to do to prepare yourself, and you have released yourself to Me. All things will flow, and never stop to judge, for what you might think in your earthly consciousness has not touched anyone, could very well have touched someone very deeply. If you come and always ask that your brothers receive something—whatever can help them—then it is placed before them. And if they have even a half-willingness to accept, they will be blessed. Never judge. Just come before Me and always be willing to be the empty vessel, and allow those things to be poured forth to bless your brothers. That is what I would have you do, and that is what you have also desired to do. Go forth doing this, knowing that you are always supported, taken care of, by Me. Never have a doubt. If I tell you, "Go here or there," just go. And it may simply be to smile or give a kind word to someone on the sidewalk. But the trip you have made will not have been in vain, for I will always take you where there are those who can be blessed.

What should the focus of further writing be?

As you were instructed, and is included in the first volume, share with your brothers your experiences, for in sharing those experiences you have had with Me, they are inspired themselves, particularly those who may have thought that they might for some reason not be worthy, so that they may know that there is no such thing as unworthiness. There is no *one who has fallen so low that, if deep within his heart, he desires Me and turns toward Me, the way is not open and he will not be received. This cannot happen. So, share more and more of those experiences to help your brothers feel that they are also at home in My Presence—that they may come before Me—and that there is great blessing when they desire to come before Me asking for another brother or sister, so that they also may participate in this great time of harvest. Just share, and as you sit down to write, come before Me, and surely, **surely**, I will place those ideas into your mind. I will give you the words, the words that will touch their hearts. Never doubt. Have no concerns about this. Just come, asking, "Father, inspire us once again, for we need this—everyday."*

The Heavenly Father is asked to please speak of what the vessel may need to do in order to be best prepared for Your service in the future?

Do not consider that there is one plan set in stone that cannot be changed. What would be in accordance with My Will and fulfill your purpose on earth can be done under different scenarios, and as time goes on the possibilities may change, adapting themselves to choices that you, as well as your brothers in the world, may make. Just come each day before me and say, "Help me, Father, that I remember always to look to You, and use me as Your vessel, whether I am aware of it or not, so that my brothers may be blessed through me. And even when my personality is reacting, may that reaction be that response my brother may need at that point—so that he never be harmed by me and my ignorance." And then allow Me from day to day, week to week, to lead you wherever I would have you led. And if your plans for the day don't seem to work out, consider that it could be I have other plans, and that the detours you make may lead you to an encounter with a brother upon whom I can leave an indelible imprint, just simply by having touched the spirit deep within and awakened the heart to express that which it was created to express—My Love. Remember, wherever you go, you are My vessel, and there are those who can be touched if you allow yourself to be empty so that My blessings can flow through.

Some have said that Jesus laughed, even on the way to Gethsemane and at the cross. What was he laughing about?

He had great humor, and even when the circumstances and situations are very grim, there is often a place for humor— things that can be done that, even when everything seems so serious, can awaken humor. For remember, He was not threatened. He knew that He was My Son. And He also knew that His brothers and sisters were My children also—even though there seemed to be a veil across the doorway to the heart, that did not allow the Light through. And those whom He touched, even as He was being crucified, have not forgotten. And with such joy in one's heart, how can one not laugh? Go forth, and desire to be another such son or daughter of Mine.

Is there any other helpful advice for the vessel as to how to maximize abilities to bring through messages or how best to connect with those who could benefit from such messages?

Be patient. Wait upon the Lord. And while you are waiting, rejoice in the Father. Rejoice that your Father is Love, and not such a God as many of the ancient cultures perceived God as being, but a God of Light and Purity—a God of Holiness. And seek each day to be His vessel in whatever way He chooses at that time. Seek not to rush, or to enter a door before you reach the threshold. For the Father leads you step by step, moment by moment, and there is perfection, there is holiness, in every moment, wherever you may be—even when someone has irritated you, or the traffic jam is trying your patience. Remember, if you are sitting there and can't move, you can always think of the Father and His Light, and extend His Light and Love. It is an opportunity that is being given to you, whereas if your actions were not ever obstructed, you would not have that moment of quiet and peace. And remember, those who are closely connected with the Father and His blessed Son have a sense of humor and an abundance of joy, and they look upon each one they encounter as the Father come in a different way, to be recognized and to be greeted in a manner that bespeaks His Holiness and His Love.

Any further message the Father might have is requested at this time.

You should be aware that there is a great host of beings, angelic beings and others—great prophets of the past—who are in close proximity to you on earth at this time. They are extending their love to each of you and urging that you accept to be the vessels of Love and of Light. For they have great desire to also participate and have great interest in the outcome of this harvest. Each one of them would desire that not one soul fail to come forth and ask to be harvested. There is a great host there. They support you in My Name, and you could never be alone. Not only could you never be alone because you are an extension of Myself, but you are not alone because there are so many others of your brothers who vibrate with the same frequency of Light and Love, and who rejoice in each deed, each act of kindness, each thought that you have of recognizing and appreciating a brother. If you really knew the size of this host, you would realize what a great privilege it is for you to be on earth at this time, and what a great responsibility it is that you not fail, even once, to do all that you could to allow your brothers to be blessed, to be inspired. Keep this in mind, and know also (suddenly the Master made His Presence known, and the radiance of joy and love emanating from Him was breathtaking) your Brother and Master, Jesus, is always there. He has always been there. He never left the earth. He extends His Love, and he rejoices in every good deed, just as I do. He is always there—always there with Me! Never forget, He is in your heart. You should never, ever, be disheartened or have a doubt of any kind. Just remember, He is there, and turn and say, "Dear Master, encourage us, lift us up to the Father, and help us," and just know that this happens. He is there, and he blesses you. He extends his arms, He touches you, and He embraces you. What greater comfort could you have? You are not comfortless. He promised you that you would not be comfortless (see John 14:18), and He never fails on a promise. Remember, just always remember! And if something helps you to remember better, such as wearing a cross, or anything else that reminds you of Him—keeping a picture that someone has painted of Him near you—then use that to remind you. Such tools are not to be looked down upon. They help you, for anything that reminds you of Him and Myself is of benefit to you and all your brothers.

Then the Master himself in an ever so soft and gentle voice spoke.

Go in peace. Bring Me, and My Father, to your brothers. Take every opportunity. Seize the moment. Never neglect. For I showed you the way. You need only follow and be another such one blessed by the Father because you have chosen, elected, to be blessed. And I stand ever beside you with My arms around you. I take you with Me before His Throne, and He blesses us together.

MESSAGE ABOUT VICARIOUS SUFFERING

MESSAGE ABOUT VICARIOUS SUFFERING

The Heavenly Father is asked to speak of vicarious suffering. Is there such a thing? If so, explain how it can be beneficial to take away the suffering of people whose souls have taken it on as a means of evolving towards realization of the Divine Spirit within them. Is it not robbing them of opportunities? Do they no longer need these experiences?

You should not concern yourself with suffering that you might take upon you for the sake of others. You come into My Presence with great love in your heart for all your brothers. And you may come with them one by one. As you come before Me with great love—because you desire that each one know and experience My Love as you have known and experienced It, and with deep compassion as you see their great suffering brought about by having strayed away and lost sight of My

Vision, My Love, My Light—as you do this, acknowledging the Purity and Holiness of Myself in each one, you lose sight of anything you might previously have looked upon as less than perfect or less than whole—anything that might have needed healing, as it might have been so labeled. In acknowledging My Spirit in your brother, you touch the spirit in him, and there comes about an embrace—a holy embrace between you and him.

And as you stand before Me, asking that all blessings that can be bestowed upon the brother be given in the appropriate way—as you volunteer to be yourself the vessel through which, if it is appropriate, any blessings may flow—then you have yourself done the very most important thing that you could do so that your brothers may receive their release. Then it could be that I may lay upon your heart something that you need to do, but keep in mind that you must be very patient, for your brother may not yet be ready to receive those blessings I hold in store for him. Now, do bear in mind that there are many brothers who are touched by the suffering of other brothers and desire to be of help to them, and they may do whatever seems possible to them in the moment. If they have not yet learned to recognize My Spirit within and to release all things to Me, and they are in some way able to take upon themselves the suffering of other brothers, it is a sign of their great love for their brothers that they may do so. And it is perhaps a test of their own desire for oneness—to look beyond themselves in love for their brothers. If they should desire to do so, each one accepts to be helpful to his brothers in whatever way they can accept on their journey.

But, as you come before Me, also keep in mind that you ask that My Will be done, and you ask for what is appropriate for your brother. And have no desire that something should be lifted from your brother if it still serves a purpose—a purpose that will eventually lead him directly into the knowledge and recognition of My Light and My Love that is within his heart, and into the knowledge that he rests in My arms. Have no fear—all things that are beneficial to him will be given, and those things that are not will not be given. Nothing will be taken away that serves the purpose of leading him to recognition of Me and recognition that I am manifest as his brother. So, accept to be a vessel, and accept the ways that I bless your brothers through you. Just relax and leave all things to Me. Allow My Love to well up within your heart. It could be that as you come with a brother the only appropriate thing in that moment may be just to extend your love, touch your brother—and let him know, deep within, the love you have for him. So can you be My vessel. So can you serve your brothers who have lost their way—who have turned away from the Light and been distracted, and simply need to be gently turned back in the right direction.

So, the issue is not really suffering as much as it is turning towards the Light?

Suffering, as it is perceived by you on earth, is simply a means. There are those times when your brothers bring it upon themselves by having violated holy laws, but it also serves to cause them to turn, seeking in the direction from whence only true help can come. As long as they are complacent in the idle joys and thrills of life on earth—and are not in harmony with Divine Love in their hearts—there can be suffering because, until they reach a point where they finally cannot help themselves, they will not turn to the Light. For those, some suffering can be a tremendous blessing, but the issue is not suffering—the issue is facing the Light, and realizing their identity is a Light and a Love that can only be experienced—it cannot be explained.

Is there a benefit to the one who has taken on the suffering vicariously? If not, why is the suffering necessary?

To those who have perhaps taken on suffering from someone else, the benefit would be that they have allowed such compassion to well up within their hearts that they are willing to accept anything in order to be of assistance to another brother. And in so caring for another brother, they lose sight of themselves, and they stop thinking about what they might find uncomfortable or distasteful. Their greatest desire is to have the light in another brother's heart become unveiled and expand, so that they may be allowed to gaze upon it and have the great joy of recognizing the Father as He is come to them as that person. So, it can serve for some who are learning to love their brothers as much as themselves. They can, however, grow into an understanding of how their brothers can be helped in the greatest way possible. Never condemn or judge others who are trying to help, should you in your own mind perceive that this might not be the greatest way. Just look at their hearts and the Light within and ask that they may be helped to recognize in all cases what is the most beneficial way for them. That will be your service—an expression of your love for them.

So, the point is in the loving, not in the suffering?

Yes, you should not desire simply to suffer. There may have been some in the past who have seen suffering as what they should strive for—that it is necessary to suffer in order to come to a knowledge of the Father. This is not the most beneficial way that they can experience and know the Father; however, the desire to know Me enough to be willing to suffer has itself shown that they are seeking to fully know My Presence. As you on earth may blunder about, be not overcome or saddened by some of the dead-end streets you go into. It is a part of the process, and by going through the process you have experiences through which you can identify with your own brothers. By being able to identify with that, your compassion and love is increased, and any tendency you might have to ever judge them falls away. If you have not had any of their experiences, and do not know their suffering, then you do not understand your brothers, and you may be inclined to simply say, "Father, bless them," and then go your way. But you must stand there and say, "Father, is there something I can do, is there some way that I can allow You to express through me?" and be willing to take that on yourself. Unless you are willing to go out into the byways of the earth—wherever I may lead you—then you have not recognized that as long as there is one brother who is lost and cannot find the way, but who is desiring to find the way and could be helped—as long as there is one left—your joy could not be full.

So, the benefit of suffering would be that you would be less likely to judge another—that suffering would help you to stay away from judgment—reject judgment—and instead embrace joining with the brother, and it would let the brother know that you are joining with him?

Never just choose to suffer. Just be willing to accept whatever the process is into which the Father may choose to lead you. Do not perceive it as suffering, even though it may appear to be a hardship. Always know that there is a Divine Purpose to what happens—once you have released yourself to the Father and accepted that only His Will be done. It is necessary that you do that. If you should take upon yourself to decide what another brother needs, you must realize that you cannot know that. You must allow the Father to do it. The suffering of your brother may be necessary to some extent in order to bring him to a point where he realizes that he has lost his way and cannot help himself, and then turns to Me. The most important thing for your brothers walking in darkness—who have lost their way—is to reach a point where they turn to Me and say, "Help me, just provide a way. Help me." For having once turned, they are then going in the right direction.

So, in some sense, to engage in vicarious suffering might be a kind of human insistence on a solution that is not God's solution; in fact that we cannot know God's solution. We simply must be open to it. In other words, vicarious suffering is another way that we might try to solve another person's dilemma from our perspective. Is that correct?

Yes, and you do not have the wisdom to know what is the best solution. Sometimes, the brother may need to suffer a little while longer, and sometimes that may not be the case. You do not know and cannot make that decision. There are some brothers of yours who have great healing ability, and can take away the suffering of your brothers. They do not have the knowledge of whether or not this is appropriate at that time. They can also take some of the negativity upon themselves, but it does not have to be done this way—there is another way. But do not judge a brother who does this, because it is a sign of great compassion in his heart that he would be willing to take this upon himself. Just come before Me and say, "This brother has such great compassion, and yet is bringing so much upon himself. I ask, dear Father, that You help him to know that he should always turn to You, and whatever You should tell him is the appropriate way, is the way it should be done, for of himself he cannot know.

Would the Father give some instruction as to what the vessel should be doing at this time?

As you go about your daily life, never be upset or concerned when everything goes topsy-turvy, because I have other plans at times. Just always know that what I have decided is the perfect thing to happen will come about, and you will be led into places where you come in contact with others whom I can touch through you. You may never be aware of it. There may never be a word spoken—there may just simply be touching the energy of another person that may lift some sorrow, distress, or depression. Your job is to simply be empty, and you will not know My Presence fully unless you are empty, for as I flow through you, you are also blessed. If you decide what must be done, you have closed the door—you will not feel My Presence, and your brothers will not be blessed in the greatest way possible—you have restricted them. As you rise in the morning, say, "Father, this day help me that I may always look to You and always be empty; and bless my brothers, whether I know it or not, in whatever way is best for them. Help me to always accept to be led wherever you would lead me." And when I lay it upon your heart, be willing to drop those mundane things and pause a moment to receive the instruction or message I have, or to extend your love to someone you may think about, because I put the thoughts into your mind. You know there are brothers in other parts of the world who are suffering terribly and who are also seeking a way of love. Just extend your love and know that it flows through you and touches them. Although you may never know or see anything discernible, judge it not, for a blessing has been given, and you have been the vessel through which it was given. You have fulfilled your purpose.

Some people say that they find it difficult to see the Father in all things they encounter, and sometimes we seem to take another person's suffering upon ourselves and even have difficulty sleeping at night. Can any help be given?

It is certainly possible that when you look upon other brothers, it wrenches your heart, and you have great desire to lift that suffering. In a way, you suffer with them because of your love, but always remember My Light—My Spirit—within them, and focus your attention upon it to the point that you begin to see that Light only, and the suffering melts away because you see it no more—you look through it—and you feel the Love that is Mine. Embrace what is holy within your brothers, and continue to do that. As you look upon them, it is certainly appropriate, when you see dark clouds around them, to just gently remove them saying, "Father, all that is not in accordance with Your Will for my brother at this time, if he permits, I will remove. I place it over Your Flame of Love beside me, so that it may burn away all the dross and release the pure and holy energy." And then you bless your brother, and you focus always on the Holiness within him—the Beauty and the Light you see there. And each time you do that, you awaken it more in him; but remember, your brother is Myself, come to you to bless you, and what you may perceive as suffering is only a perception—not that you should ignore it, but do not allow it to make your heart heavy. Release it to me.

Then take your brother by the hand, put your arm around him, and come before My Presence and say, "Holy Father, I bring one so dear to me! I love him! I desire that he know Your Love as I do! We come before you. Bless us together, and allow all that is not true and real, that is only a perception, that is an ignorance or a lack of knowledge of You, to just melt away as we stand before You gazing into the Light. Know that I love my brother. I cannot be filled with joy unless I know that he knows it also." And then release all that is heavy on your heart and know that what is heavy on his heart will also, when it is appropriate, be released. Be not disheartened if it is not released from him totally in that moment. Just rejoice that I know, in all My Love and Gentleness, when it is totally appropriate, and it will be done, for I have total love for your brothers—I will bring that about in the perfect way. So, as he stands with you before Me and gazes into the Light—as he allows the Light of the Spirit within to beam from his eyes—he is released of all things. Then he also has that great desire to go back into the world as one like unto yourself who wants to gather together all those who are willing and bring them to Me. When you do this, you release all things to Me, and you are blessed with your brother—you know My Love and Light welling up within you, and you realize that I am manifest as you in the world.

You have come forth into the world to be another one to help many brothers here, not by taking their troubles upon yourself, but by bringing them to me and watching them be transformed into pure Light. I walk the earth each day as you—I touch your brothers as you—and you have a holy service here on earth each moment of the day—even as you sleep. If you have accepted that purpose and have the intention that My Light go through you, I will bless the world—even the earth itself, so that it may be transformed and no longer be known as the planet of suffering and agony, but the planet where Love and Light radiates out into the whole universe. Those in distant galaxies will look in wonder and say, "What a beautiful star that is! There is so much light coming to us from it. How did this come about?" They will want to know how all this was transformed. You are blessed!

Is there a closing message?

The Master spoke:
Go forth in the Light—knowing that you rest in the Light—knowing the Light goes through you—having one great desire that the Father help you to always be totally empty, so that no brother who could be helped would fail to receive help because you perhaps have not been open, but rather that you always be an empty vessel, and those around you be blessed. Never stop to question, and never wonder about it. Just know that because you have asked Me to be in your heart—to

express through you—I walk the earth as you. Did I not tell you I would come again? I just didn't explain how it would be. I walk the earth as you when you allow it—then you are Me. Just ask each day, "Master, be me. Help me to allow You to be me." That is all you need to do. Don't get bogged down with wondering about it. Just have that intention and ask, and be open. Allow your brothers to be blessed as each one comes to you—just reach forth to that Light in their hearts, desiring to touch it and be enthralled by it. Assure them of the Light there. If you try to figure it out or focus on appearances, you close the door. You must release the perceptions in order to know My embrace.

Allow the Love to flow through you as you speak to your brothers, for it is only in this way that they will allow the shackles to fall away. Allow your perceptions of lack of love and of pain to fall away as you focus on the Light and Love in their hearts—allow those things to dissolve. And when you focus totally upon the Light and Love, and they see that you are seeing only That within them—and not seeing their pain and suffering—that is what allows them also to release those things. For if you look upon them in pity, they will notice your perception of that which allows pity. Go beyond pity, for compassion and love flow across all things. Then you allow Me to be in you, and you see Me in your brother. And you look into his heart and say, "I thank you, Father, that You sent this brother to me, so that I might gently part those clouds and gaze upon Your purity in his heart, and allow those other things to drop away in love." I bless you, My dear brother, and I thank you that you allow Me to walk the earth in you.

A RELUCTANT SOUL ACCEPTS TO COME TO EARTH

A RELUCTANT SOUL ACCEPTS TO COME TO EARTH

The point has been reached when I am about to be sent to earth, but having seen the cruelty, violence, and suffering on earth, I am very resistant to leaving the celestial realms. I say, "I have a great desire to be in the Presence of Jesus, to know the Holy Light of the Father, and to go beyond the many processes that seem so endless and the experiences of suffering that seem so meaningless."

I come into the Presence of Jesus, and He poses the question, *"Do you care for your brothers as much as you care for yourself?"*

I say, "It bothers me much—they suffer so terribly. I think something needs to be done."

Jesus says, *"There is something. Would you care to help?"*

I look at him with great admiration and appreciation for all He has done for us, and I say, "I'll do anything you ask because of my great love for you."

He says, *"What is needed the most—the way that you can help the most—is for you to go to earth."*

I cringe somewhat and say, "It's so painful."

He says, *"Just trust me. I will be with you. It is through volunteering to help others that you will also lift the memories of suffering you yourself have experienced, and you will go beyond them. And you will know that you rest in the Light. You will know joy. There are many brothers on earth who are also asking for help and who need someone to come, but, in order to be of the most help, you must be willing to just go and do what the Father places before you, and to allow Him to guide you and show you the way. I will be with you, but if you decide that you need to know yourself what your brothers need, and that relief from suffering is all that is necessary, you will limit what can be done because there is a great complacency that comes about in some souls if there is nothing but enjoyment, living in the sunshine, and playing. In order for them to come to the experience of knowing the Father, they must desire it, and some will have to be put in situations where they realize that they must ask for something else—something greater. A complacency is there that numbs them, and they will never desire to go beyond this until they have situations come to them where they are somewhat uncomfortable and are not able to solve the problems themselves.*

You must trust that the Father knows what is best and allow Him to lead you. You must be totally empty, and He will flow through. Allow Him to touch them in the way that only He knows is the way that will be helpful and cause a great desire to be awakened in their hearts to come into His Presence—to know that they rest in His Arms and there is nothing to fear. There is a need for some brothers to come—to volunteer to do this. Should you desire to do it, it would be out of your love for them and your desire to help—even if it is uncomfortable to do so—and your desire to walk in the way that I show you and be the Father's servant. So, the choice is yours. You may be a helper, or you may rest here and risk becoming complacent and looking upon your brothers and saying, "May God provide you a way," without volunteering to be an instrument through which that way is provided. And you must decide."

I look at Him. I am deeply moved and I say, "I will go, but I'm not sure that I can do this unless I am confident and know that I can feel Your Presence—feel Your nearness; otherwise, I fear that I will lose the way myself."

He says, "*I have never failed you on a promise. I am always there. Remember, you yourself may have to go through some experiences where you feel great despair—where you feel lost and you feel you cannot find Me and the Father—so that on earth you can identify with your brothers and know how they feel. You will have a compassion that is so great you will release all the other enticements—things that bring you personal and private joy. You realize that your real joy is the fulfillment of being a child of the Father—reaching out your hands to your brothers in the manner in which I showed you and allowing the Father to flow through you. For only in being empty can you be the Father's vessel truly—dependable and with no hindrance—so that nothing your brother may need will fail to be offered to him."*

I realize how difficult it is going to be and that also I wouldn't choose anything else. So, I embrace Him and allow Him to infuse me with His Love. I say, "I thank You that You loved us so much, and You took on so much to help us. Help me that I may also be able to help in such a way, so that all that could happen is available. And now I accept Your blessing and that of the Father. I go."

He says, *"Go in peace, girded with the Light of the Father—with His Love in your heart. Go, for it is that Love and Light of the Father that is the salvation of all those who wander in darkness—who are lost in darkness! Go, allowing yourself to be led day by day—not knowing where the path may lead—and welcoming every change in the plan! Always trust that the Father has a plan and there is not likely to be even a chance encounter or a meeting that He has not arranged. Always look to the Father, always look to Me, and say, 'I thank You, that You are with me and help me so that I may be empty and open, and keep me pure so that there may be nothing my brothers need that is not able to flow through. For I too desire that their tears be wiped away and that they may know they need only look up into the Light and rejoice in the Father—that they may give thanks—and may always be aware that they rest in the Light and the Love, and may join in the brotherhood of those who come—if need be, even come back a thousand times, so that there may be not one soul left who is unattended.'"*

I now see that my joy cannot be full if I know there is one wandering in the darkness and, if there is even the slightest chance that his gaze may be attracted and enticed to turn and face the Light, I may be able to see the smile on his face, be witness to the gleam of hope in his eyes, experience his embrace, and feel my heart merge with his in the Light and the Joy of the Father as His Love wells up within both of us as one heart. And we will then sing praises to the Father and give thanks to our glorious Master that He has encouraged us to participate in this activity that causes darkness to disappear as one more soul accepts to open the door to his heart and allow one of us to glimpse the Purity the Father has gently laid there—has protected from all of the appearances and perceptions that once clouded it and caused it to lose hope, so that we get a glimpse—knowing that this *is* walking in the Presence of the Father Himself. For He did not create by partitioning Himself—separating Himself from what He created—but created by extending Himself and indwelling all. I will also give thanks that I may now be on earth and know that I walk in the Presence of the Father and may no longer label the earth as a God-forsaken place. I lift up my eyes to the Father and say, "I thank You that You have created a place where my brothers can go and have the opportunity to have the scales lifted from their eyes, so that they also may rejoice in the Light—and walk in the Light."

And now I look into the eyes of the Master. I put my hands on His arms and say, "Thank you for awakening me to this cause that is blessed by You and the Father—and has a holy purpose. I go with joy in my heart." He embraces me, and as I turn to embark on the journey, He places His hands on my shoulders and gives one last message.

"Remember, whenever you turn to Me and ask for the Presence of the Father, and you feel that someone has touched you on the shoulder, it is I, and I am there with you wherever you go—no matter how the situation around you may appear to be as you walk among lost souls who wallow in darkness. I am there with you. I will never forsake you. Anytime you ask to feel My Love and the Father's well up in you and touch your brothers, know that it will happen, and they will be touched in some way—whether they are aware of it or not. If you ask for another brother, blessings will be given—they cannot fail to be given. Should you choose to do so, every moment of your life can be a blessing to your brothers, whether you are in their presence or not, just by your thinking about them. Anytime you are going on a journey or think of a far and distant land—you think of brothers there and how they have fallen into ways that are lacking in love and are expressing their own despair— feelings of being lost—what you need to do is say, 'Father, extend your love through me and my heart. Touch them. Provide each one a way somehow.' Then know that even if they don't accept it in their lives on earth, they will receive a blessing some way in spirit in eternity. Your true purpose is

this. There is no greater purpose—you could not choose a greater one. And you can also, with the desire in your heart, be a constant blessing every moment—even as you sleep, for the desire of your heart never sleeps. Have great joy in your choice. And now, dear brother, go! We watch over you."

And so I embark on the journey.

Now in reviewing the past events of the life on earth, all the unpleasant things—even the experiences of despair—melt away. And they are forgotten, for I now know that they are the means of learning to identify with my brothers to such an extent that I would offer everything. There is no greater desire, no greater joy or fulfillment—even no other joy—than to be one who is empty—to be one through whom the true Light and Joy of the Father is flowing and touches those around me—and to realize that going into the great pit of despair was necessary so that the love and compassion within me would not cringe and turn away, and say, "Father, I just cannot look upon it." I will put my arms on their shoulders willingly and walk there with them, and see them as they feel totally despicable and hate themselves—be able to be in a physical body and look into their physical eyes and say, "I'm not really aware of those things. What I am aware of is what is in your heart. I see a light so pure that there is nothing else to see. Believe me, I see you only as God's holy child. Just open your heart and accept my embrace, so that those things that cause you despair may fall away as a garment and disappear, and you may also know yourself in the Light—a Light that has its anchor in the Father's Heart. For my greatest desire is that you know the Father—His Light and His Love—as I do. My joy would not be full if I thought you were wandering in darkness." I put my arms around him, and I go to the Master and the Father and say, "Look whom I've brought with me. Look at my beautiful brother—how he shines! And there is joy in his heart!" And I say to the Father, "Thank you for creating him."

I may then return again to go into the byways and find another one who has reached the point where he calls out, "Father, just send someone, someone to touch me." Now I know what my calling is and what my fulfillment is. It is my joy. And by participating in this, I walk in Light, I walk in Love, and I do not feel separated from it. "I thank you for every opportunity—that opportunities abound. And also I ask for my brothers that they have infinite opportunities to choose over and over again—no matter how many opportunities, there are never too many—so that all creation may be filled with Light and Love and the earth fulfill its mission—even though it may have groaned in the past with all the sorrow—and actually gets to laugh and dance, and to rejoice in all the opportunities it has provided."

He is urging me, "*Walk in the Light!*"

GOD'S GIFT OF
CRYSTALS AND STONES

GOD'S GIFT OF CRYSTALS AND STONES

For those who may think that wearing crystals and stones in order to benefit from their vibrations is hocus pocus, I would remind them that Aaron, the High Priest of Israel, wore a breastplate that was set with onyx and other stones. (See Ex 25:7) I don't think it is likely that, for a group of people wandering in the wilderness, this was for show alone. The following message was given to me about stones.

Now let it be known that the Father extends blessing to you and your brothers through crystals and stones, as well as through many other means. There are very subtle vibrations that may touch you in a way you are not consciously aware of, and also there are vibrations that you receive and perceive visually, which you may be aware of, that bring balance to some part of your being. All of these crystals and stones, being the creation of the Father's Nature, have the ability to bring His balancing and healing Energy to you.

The stones are a part of the Father's creation, and as you know, all parts of creation can be a great delight for you and can bring joy and a sense of well-being to you—such as plants that you might eat and they nourish you. Just go with the feeling—if you get up in the morning and you feel attracted to a particular stone, take that one, love it, carry it with you, and appreciate the individuality of the expressions of the Father's Being that comes forth in this unique form. It brings enrichment to your life and helps you also to remember to rejoice in all things the Father brings to you, for all things that you encounter are Himself.

(Although the descriptions of the energies given below would apply to the particular stone that was being held at the time the information was received, it is reasonable to assume that most of it would apply to all stones of that category.)

AMETHYST

This a stone that has a quality you would feel as energy—an energy that quickens the spirit and would inspire you to desire to share the gifts of the Father with your fellowman—even to the extent of sharing your experiences with the Father. For in sharing these things, your brothers might be inspired to themselves seek to allow that which seems to close them off to be removed, so that they, too, may also enter into those experiences—experiences that, even at times, are difficult to verbalize because they are experiences of things of which many brothers on your earth have no conception.

AMETHYSTS (on a string)

These are stones of lightness and gentle joy—stones that radiate light and lovingness into the world and make your brothers feel blessed when they feel it. It is really a broad smile.

AMETRINE (large)

There is a gentle love in this stone, a rather subtle love, but it is a stone that would bring to you some patience, long-suffering, forbearance, in going about your tasks on earth and in interacting with your other brothers, some of whom may appear to you to have a natural talent for bringing out the worst in you. So, make this stone your companion. It will allow you to touch them and bring out the best in them.

AMETRINE (on a string)
These are stones of responsibility—responsibility that is taken on with a certain seriousness, but stones that encourage you to rightness of mind and thoughts. For there are times in your experience when you must take responsibility to see that certain things are done for the benefit of your brothers and yourself.

AQUAMARINE (small size, light blue)
Now, this particular stone has more vibration than the azurite (see below), a stronger energy. It is an energy of light, somewhat cheerful, and it would be good to wear when energy seems to be a bit low, or when one might seem to be perhaps depressed—or not so cheerful himself. There is a very gentle sort of chuckle about it.

AQUAMARINE (chips on a string, medium blue)
There is a certain humor here. It is a little bit of a heavy humor—it is not a light humor—but it would certainly help you to feel grounded in the earth, to relate to your brothers, and be a bit jovial.

AQUAMARINE (cubes on a string, very light in color)
These stones help you to be the point—the apex—of a vortex of light as it streams into the earth, so that it may come down to you as a point from which it can be extended into the world. It broadens your outer consciousness so that it may accept from all directions this light coming in to you.

AVENTURINE WITH SOME EMERALD INTERSPERSED (on a string)
These are stones that dissolve negative vibrations, and, therefore, are cleansing and allow a feeling of rejuvenation because, as the negativity is released and disappears, and the positive light comes in, one feels renewed and can therefore go about fulfilling his function on earth.

AZESTULITE QUARTZ

This is a stone of the joy of the fullness of Spirit, the fullness of the knowledge of the Father, Who walks forth into the world extending joy to your brothers and allowing them to see that, no matter what comes, when one's attention is focused upon Him, there is only joy.

AZURITE

The energies of this stone appear to be very subtle and gentle, somewhat as a gentle breeze.

BLOODSTONE

This is a stone of peace, a peace that passes understanding if you can allow it to vibrate in harmony with your being—Peace of the Father that comes when all fear is released and when you know through your experience of the Father that He walks beside you. For He is always there, and no matter what comes your way, it is a blessing, and there is only blessing and good to come from it. And there is a peace in your heart and your soul as you walk through those experiences.

CARNELIAN (on a string)

Should you desire and choose to wear these stones, you need merely say, "Father, send forth all blessings that are appropriate through these stones, that they may emanate constantly, so that there never be a moment when I do not feel those vibrations that You send to me." For these stones are themselves as vessels. They are waiting for you to ask them to be blessed through Me. For if you do not ask, they are not allowed to fulfill their purpose to the fullest. So, always ask, and then you will notice how they radiate with the light, that your asking of Me has allowed to flow through them, and bless you.

CELESTITE

When wearing this stone you will feel the presence of those the Father sends, for he sends many to you in physical form or in more subtle form to allow you to know, to experience, His Love coming through other individualized beings. He also sends blessings through these forms—even takes care of the needs for your physical experience. And you may even, if you listen attentively, think that you hear the rustle of wings.

CHLORITE

This stone has the comforting element of a loving pet, similar to the cat that might come and rub against your ankles. You feel the love and know it cares. You know that this animal is happy that you are there and that the love from that animal is unconditional. And this stone also brings that vibration so that you may feel and know that the energies of the universe are loving and beneficial to you, that they are without condition, and that you can feel secure on the earth where there might appear to be insecurity and so much turmoil around you. This stone helps you to feel that security.

CITRINE

This is a stone of loveliness, a stone of sweetness and gentleness. It has a vibration that is healing to your brothers, for through the vibration of this stone they experience that you truly appreciate them and their true reality and are in no way influenced by opinions of other people, including opinions they may have about themselves. There is just a gentle sweetness there that has such healing quality it is difficult to explain.

DANBURITE

This stone has the quality of flowing water that stimulates gently and gives a feeling of aliveness, a feeling of being washed and feeling clean, and ready to express joy.

EMERALD (embedded in a glossy black rock)

There is a brightness here somewhat like a musical piece played in D-major. It is a brightness of sunshine and everything being clean, washed, optimistic, so that you may go forth undaunted by conditions that seem stressful or distressing. This keeps you from being drawn down by those experiences and situations—a good substitute for Saint John's Wort.

EMERALDS (on a string)

These are stones of light that seems to part any darkness and to cause any disturbing mask to fall away. The feeling is very light, as a cloud gently floating by.

EMERALD, (RED EMERALD)

This is a stone with a softness of bringing hope, also even delight, in an innocent and childlike way. So, if there are times when you may look upon situations around you and think, "There is no escape, no hope," just wearing this gentle stone will help you to remember that there is hope for light and love, and it will surely cause you to smile more often during the day when you wear it.

FLUORITE (yellow)

This stone would help you to learn to love with the innocence of a child or pet—without judgments—or loving without seeking love in return, but expressing love because it is your natural expression—it wells up within your heart. And it blesses those around you, for as the vibrations flow across them, it cleanses and heals those things that have caused them distress—and yet it is not overwhelming. It is very subtle and comforting, but always reassuring because it does not fail—does not go away.

GOLD-INFUSED QUARTZ

This stone transforms energies that are not at the present expressing in their most positive and beneficial way. It removes those things that are not positive—or turns the direction of the energies into that which will express vibrations of light and love. It is helpful for those who desire to be transformed and to accept to be that which they were created.

GOLDEN BERYL-AQUAMARINE-QUARTZ (on a string)
These stones bring a mingling of energies, which can be focused and harmonized by your intent. It is necessary that you have an intention to do so and to set a purpose for what the energies would help you to accomplish, for it is as if a host is there at your disposal to help you, but you must ask and you must delineate in order for them to be of assistance to you.

HELIODOR (GOLDEN BERYL)
This is a stone of hope, a stone that allows you and your brothers to release those things that have caused you to lose hope. It represents a hope that sees there is light at the end of the tunnel, a hope that sees this light beckoning to them. As they walk through the trials of the problems of their lives, it helps them to always gaze at that light and not let their gaze stray right or left, but single-mindedly travel toward the light with great hope.

JADE

There is a lightness as of clouds of light that appear to have no weight about them, and wearing this would make you feel that you glide across the earth; so if there are times when responsibilities are heavy, this would make things seem lighter as you go about doing those things that are put before you each day.

KYANITE

This stone has a blissful-like, loving quality to it. It is more than a chuckle. This one is a laugh. It brings sunshine into the hearts of those where everything appears to be clouded. So, it is particularly good to have with you when you come to your brothers who are suffering and depressed, and all seems so dismal.

LAPIS LAZULI (with some pyrite)

There is a great depth about this stone that gives a feeling of being anchored, which would be helpful when you feel that you are being tossed about and need to feel being secure and anchored, even to feel grounded—having a sense of stability.

LEMURIAN SEED QUARTZ CRYSTAL

This is a stone with a natural radiance of light, a light that rejoices and lifts you up as you walk your pathway on earth. This is a light that shines away darkness, and as you wear it, if you allow, its light will merge with yours, and those about you who are open to seeing this will note the radiance by which your own radiance has been enhanced through wearing this stone.

LITHIUM-INCLUDED QUARTZ

This stone would help you to feel in harmony with nature—the gentle breezes, the sunshine, and the grasses as they sway in the wind. It is a stone that can bring balance to you to keep the heaviness of responsibilities from weighing you down. It is a stone of lightheartedness with a gentle joy—a joy that you would think you feel when the gentle wind blows through your hair, and you hear the birds singing.

MOLDAVITE (small thin piece)

If there are times when there is a need to express the energy of the Father's Heart, this is a stone that would be good to wear, for there is not only the connection with the Father, but also a knowing that there is no lack in His abundance, there is no lack in energy, time, or anything else needed to perform any activities that are placed before you.

MOLDAVITE (medium in size)
This is another stone of light—of lightness and of light—that would help you so that you walk the earth, but your feet barely touch it. And in going about with this energy you bring much joy, and you are not weighted down by all the excess baggage that so many of your brothers carry. It keeps you from being dragged down by their baggage, as well as some you may have had of your own, so that you may then truly be free to be the Father's vessel of Light and Love. This stone actually almost suspends you. It lifts you up.

MOLDAVITE (rather large)
This is a stone that extends out into the night sky—deep out into the cosmos—a stone that encompasses vast regions of creation and makes you feel close to—and a brotherhood with—that which is really at a great distance.

Question: Would this particular stone be of assistance in bringing messages to people?

Yes, this stone would be helpful, for it would lift you above the structures of your world, which have blinded your eyes and at times have robbed you of your laughter and your humor, for it helps you to have a stronger connection with that which is in harmony with your true being, and it would help to make you a conduit for bringing those vibrations from higher realms into the earth. It would bless you—it would bless the aura of your body—and make you feel more in a state of harmony. It may be placed on the crown of the head, but it would also help on the heart, and would be beneficial on the forehead, as well as on the throat to help bring forth messages with the proper wording, for the selection of the words makes all the difference in whether or not a message is accessible—makes an imprint upon the person so that he would then heed the message.

Question: Concerning the desires of this vessel to be the clearest vessel possible, would a string of moldavite chips help him to attune to God and to Jesus, and would it help in bringing through messages?

A string of these stone would help raise your vibration and your thoughts above the mundane situations of life, and therefore make it easier to commune with Me; however, the desire of the heart to come before Me, and the love of Me—of My Purity and My Being—is the strongest link, and that alone can bring you to Me. But to use other creations of Mine, such as the vibrations of stones, or even symbols that remind you of Holiness, is certainly not to be looked down upon. These may be used.

MOLDAVITE (chips on a string)
These stones will make an excellent companion as you go about some of your duties on earth that may seem to be somewhat tedious and demanding—even boring. They help you to bear your responsibilities with an inner knowingness that each thing you do, can, with your desire and permission, be a great blessing to someone else. They are good companions to remind you to have this attitude as you go about the world and seek to be the instrument through which your brothers

are blessed, but keeping in mind that you may never know that many of the blessings have flowed through you. You may be totally oblivious of it, but if you have asked of Me that I bless your brothers through you, then trust—it happens, whether you know it or not!

OPALIGHT (on a string)
This is a group of stones of joy—almost bubbly joy, but rather subtle, so that it is a quiet kind of joy, but with a lightness to it—a lightness as a smile with a twinkle in the eye that can uplift the spirits of your brothers. For you are often not aware that your brothers may be depressed, and just a touch of joy with a tinge of light and love can lift the depression. You know this already because another brother told you recently—one whom you called and to whom you said, "I just want to know how you are," and his response was, "I was depressed, but you called—you just made my night." Remember, this is part of your assignment on earth—to let your brothers know that you love them and to not be hindered by social mores of interacting with people. Just say, "I love you," and don't worry about what people may think it might mean, for in lifting up the heart of a brother, you have

allowed Me to be on earth. There is nothing greater that you could do. This group of stones is a nice companion.

PETALITE (rather large)

There is a glow about this stone. It has an inner light—a light that shines, even in darkness, and gives a feeling of security and stability, and also a feeling of remembering what your mission here on earth is, so that you not be distracted, but go about being a light-bringer—that you may be your Father's vessel and your brother's helper.

PHENACITE

This has an energy similar to long blades of grass that are swaying in the wind and drinking in the sunshine, knowing that all is well, all things are provided, even though you may seem to be at a standstill. So, if there are times when you feel restless and you are not able to be held down without feeling discomfort, if you wear this stone it will help you to stay in one place attending to your task and yet know that you are drinking in the sunshine and the wind is blowing through your hair and tickling your nose.

PHENACITE (from Madagascar)

This is a stone of faith, a faith that does not allow you to forget that you have known the Father's Love and that there is nothing that stands between you and Him, and that He leads you onward always, opening doors through which you can enter and allow His Light to shine forth.

PSILOMELANE

This is a stone given to mankind to make him aware of the polarities in his experience, so that he may begin to accept the completeness in which polarities exist. For polarities are the existence of one pole and the absence of it, or lack of awareness of it, at the other pole. Where there is absence of Love or Light, there is the opportunity to bring those to remembrance, to see the Creator where He appears to be absent.

RUBY

There is here very much an energy similar to that of a butterfly, which is not only gentle but also has a patience about it as it very quietly and gently goes from one thing to another with no sense of rush or being hurried. So, if there are times in life when you feel you are chasing your tail, this is a good time to wear this stone. It will calm you down so that you glide from one task to another, and yet accomplish all things without getting too much energy in a turmoil.

RUBIES (on a string)
There is a soft and gentle joy about these stones that smiles upon you. It is contagious and makes you want to smile. It looks out upon the world and helps you to look past difficult situations and continue to smile and radiate into the earth that light that always accompanies a smile.

RUTILATED QUARTZ
This stone has a vibration similar to that of the birds that go about their daily tasks, trusting in the Father and always singing. They take what comes in life. Whether the sun shines or it rains they are always singing with joy. This stone would probably make you go about singing or humming, should you decide to wear it.

SAPPHIRE

In wearing this stone you remember more often the Holiness of the Father, the glorious Holiness of standing in His Presence and knowing that there is no other power in heaven or on earth. You remember Him so easily when you wear this stone.

SAPPHIRES (on a string)

These stones will help bring some structure as you go about your daily tasks, and they help you to be a builder as you do your part in helping the world—building it to be a better place—and helping you to know how to go about this step by step.

SODALITE

This is a stone of rejoicing with the stars as they sing with joy, joining in the chorus with the stars of the night in singing songs of appreciation and joy for the vastness of the Father's creation, and a knowing that you are connected with these distant worlds and distant sources of light—and with the heart that is within them, so that you feel as if you are a brother with the stars.

SUGILITE

This stone is somewhat like a meteor that has fallen from the skies—has dropped to the earth—and is glowing in that area where it has fallen and is bringing a sort of intense light that can cleanse situations wherever it has fallen. It is like a more direct intercession into activities, fresh and gentle—something that can be beneficial where you really need some energy and light and to cleanse something that is going on and bring it into balance.

STAUROLITE (FAIRY STONE OR FAIRY CROSS)

This stone has a vibration not as light as the yellow zincite. It also gives a feeling of well-being and being anchored in the vibrations of the earth, in the sense of knowing that there is an appropriateness of these earth vibrations and living in the earth.

SUN STONE

This stone has a more complex light that is somewhat lively—not so peaceful. It has a joyousness in motion, a liveliness about it.

TOURMALINE (dark blue)

This stone has a quiet, gentle, comforting feeling that will soothe anxieties and help you to trust the Father and the energies of the universe as you walk through the valleys of trials and temptations—and even through the valley of the shadow of death. This itself will bring you that comfort, a comfort that causes fear to melt and leaves you trusting and looking upward towards the light.

TOURMALINE (light blue)

This is a companionship stone. It helps you to feel the joy of a closer relationship with someone else—to appreciate that presence and the opportunity to extend and receive love by being in close proximity with another brother or sister.

TOURMALINE (dark olive-green)

This stone has a more intense light, similar to light of the sun, which is not harsh but would tend to help you to allow a light to radiate from your countenance, so that those who see you would remark that there is a radiance about you.

TOURMALINE (intense pink)

This stone has a sparkle about it similar to gazing into a beautiful diamond that is reflecting back light to you, and there is a sense of an inner knowing of the joy of life and the ability to allow light from your own self to shine forth and touch and bless your brothers.

TOURMALINE (very light pink)

This stone has a loving vibration about it, and there is a softness about that loving vibration, which would certainly be helpful in times when situations seem to have a little rough edge on them. It is similar to the softness of fur—quite loving.

TOURMALINE (black) INCLUSIONS IN QUARTZ

This is a stone of peace, something that is so desired and desirable on the earth at this time. This stone knows nothing other than peace. If you wear it upon your body, you will feel the vibration of peace, and as it touches that which is deep within, you feel your own inner peace rising, mingling with it, and then it will radiate from you. On such a day as you might decide to wear this stone, it could very well be that you encounter a brother who has no peace—who needs peace—and that peace will be extended to him, and he will feel it as though you have placed your arm upon his shoulder and said, "I love you, my brother, and I want you to know it. Accept this peace and this love, for it is a gift from the Father, and I allow it to be extended through me."

TOPAZ

This stone has a little of a feeling of weight to it, which perhaps would be good to use to ground yourself if you become a little bit too spaced out. For you know that you delight in taking flight to the higher realms, into the realms of the Father's Love, but remember, My child, that you are also here on the earth, and you cannot serve as well, as a vessel, if you are not in some way grounded here so that you can touch your brothers who are perhaps even more grounded, or very grounded. So this stone helps without being a heavy weight; it helps just to keep your feet on the ground.

ZINCITE, ORANGE

This stone has a somewhat grounding element about it that is not so deep as the lapis lazuli with pyrite, but gives you a center of gravity low enough in your body that you are not top-heavy and cannot be tossed about so easily. It is less heavy than the lapis but is also grounding and at the same times has some lightness of light with it, so that you feel grounded and somewhat light at the same time.

ZINCITE, YELLOW

This stone emanates a gentle, lively light, which can uplift the human spirit and just bring a sense of joy, joyous peace—a kind of quiet joy of knowing that all is well.

ZIRCON

This is a stone of elevation—as being on a mountainside lifted above situations; therefore, having some distance from them so that you can view them with some clarity and put things into focus with a greater sense of events or situations over a longer period of time, so that you know how things fit together. It gives you a distant view.

ANOTHER BOOK BY THE AUTHOR

DWELL IN LOVE
Messages for those of the heart

Jerry K. Paul

Jerry Paul asked God and Jesus for messages for those of the heart in order to inspire and instruct them as to the best way to commune with Divine Presence and discover that Presence in others. The first chapter consists of 211 daily, inspirational messages for use as devotional material. The remainder of the book consists of longer messages in answer to questions asked about healing, service, suffering, forgiveness, sacrifice, praying, how to care for the sick, the current world situation, etc. The main theme of the book is becoming an empty vessel through which God can extend unconditional love.

ORDER FORM

Please print

Name: _____

Address: _____

City: _____ State/Province: _____

Country: _____ Postal Code: _____

Telephone: (_____) _____

Please send me _____ copies of *Dwell in Love* @ $14.95* per copy.

Please send me _____ copies of *Dwell in Love II* @ $14.95* per copy.

*Add $3.50 for shipping, $1.00 for each additional copy. Alabama residents add 60 cents for state sales tax, those residing in Montgomery County add an additional 37 cents for county sales tax, and those in the city of Montgomery an additional 52 cents for city tax.

Total Amount Enclosed:

$_____(including shipping)

Please make check or money order to:

Isaiah Publications
P.O. Box 31
Pine Level, AL 36065, USA
www.dwellinlove.com